**I NEVER THOUGHT
I WOULD HAVE TO
WRITE THIS BOOK.**

-KARNES

WHEN GOODBYE BECOMES YOU

VOL. 1

ORIGINAL PROSE

-KARNES-

I never thought you would leave,
but poetry becomes those who do.
I know you may never read these
words and a part of me hopes you
never do. It would only mean you
are still okay without me.

You need to know it was always all about you. Everything I did, everything I wanted to do, everything I had planned, it was all for you. I won't ever find someone to take your place, but eventually, I will need someone who wants to stay and be a part of whatever I decide to do next. Someone who isn't a coward and runs away. Someone who communicates with me. Someone who tells me what they need. I am sorry for believing you actually fucking cared. I will not make that same mistake again. I am going to make you famous. Not because of the love you said you gave, but because of how you stopped showing it when I needed you and needed it from you the most. You will be the muse who left the sun and moon to become a mortal.

I am sorry I made you give up on me. I am sorry you felt as though you had to stop talking to me completely. I am sorry you thought you had to run away to find yourself. I am sorry I cared as much as I did and might have given you too much. I know no other way to live. I know no other way to love. I am sorry you think it is better this way. Maybe one day I will agree with your decision, but for now, I fucking hate it that you made it without me. You made it without asking me what I wanted. I guess I did teach you some things after all. I am sorry for giving you what I had learned from others my entire life. Running only gets you far enough away to see what was never going to leave you. I can no longer hope you come back. I can only hope I decide to not look back to see if you did. Once someone leaves you the way you did me, apologies are weighted down bodies never meant to breathe again or be heard from. They sit on the bottom of your spine, thinking how awful it was to lose all sense of effort and die by the sword you helped create, sharpen, and raise. If love has taught me anything, if I have learned anything from love, it is not everyone believes it to be worth the pain it gives you and it steps out from your life. I fucking believe it is all necessary to prepare you for the one who chooses to stay. The one you swear will do the same as the others did. It is when your heart is at its heaviest do you fully comprehend how much it can hold then ultimately give to someone who never asked for more than a life together. One day, someone will mean it. One day, someone won't lie about love to destroy you. One day, it will work out, because all the lies and truth of love are the same ones you carry about yourself. It takes a few encounters afterwards to gather your pieces, but you will. Love taught me all things are made of it, not just made for it.

I am done missing you. I have buried far too many in my heart and you will not have space amongst those. I cannot give you one. It would be against all that I am. I have no dead lovers buried there. It is for family and those who left me because it was their time, not mine. You will be only a viewing. No mural. No goodbye. No last song. Nothing. You already killed me once without giving a second thought to your choice of weapon. You used me against myself. You knew I couldn't do anything about it. I couldn't say anything. I couldn't even curse your fucking name. As death greets our relationship, I will look over at it and throw a handful of dirt on top of whatever it is I chose to put you in. You have brought out my darkest thoughts. You have changed my words from love and forgiveness, to death and destruction. My fingers know of this pain, as they type it out for others to read. Each strike and punch of the keys, is what the old me would have done with a wall. I would have brought the entire fucking sky down upon you for what you did to me. I understand everyone leaves at some point, but only the coldest of souls go without saying goodbye. Only one other time have I had that happen to me. You never wanted to be her or like her or do what she did to me, but now you two have more in common than ever before. You took what you needed and wanted from me, only to leave me in fucking pieces. I hope it felt good. I really fucking hope it did.

I am still trying to get over you not being here. The funny thing is, you were never really here to begin with. It is difficult for me to fathom how one can miss what was never present in one's reality. We were phone calls and messages. We were words on paper, and a few times we were colliding stars. I guess that is all we were meant to be. For the years you were in my life, I never thought you wouldn't have the guts to tell me you were leaving. After everything I told you, I never thought you would go without words and reason as to why. Your actions proved me to be wrong again. Your actions showed me just how empty you really were. All the times you thought I was cold-hearted, you trumped it all. You kept so much of yourself hidden from me. You told me it was for my safety, but now I know it was because you were keeping in the inevitable. I can only imagine everything you did behind my back when a thousand miles made us who we were. I try not to dwell on it for too long, because I become so irate and overwhelmed with anger, I honestly do not enjoy who it is I became. I would much rather go on believing we were meant for a better life together and fate came in-between us just as it brought us together. I think love is like that sometimes. I think you will see me happy one day and not say anything about it. It is how I have thought of you ever since you left me for him.

I read a quote recently that said, "when a woman leaves you for herself, she won't ever be back." I believe that to be one hundred percent true. It doesn't matter if you did anything wrong. Once she has made up her mind that the woman she wants to be, isn't who she is with you, everything else will take a backseat. The only relationship she needs is the one with herself. Maybe she thought she had it when she was with you. Maybe you thought she was happy being that version of herself. Deep down though, you knew she needed more. It wasn't that you couldn't give it to her. She simply needed it from herself. It is something I have been fighting with in my head, thinking I did something wrong, but I know in reality, once a mind is made up, there is no change. A strong, independent woman doesn't need anyone else. A vulnerable, shy, introverted woman doesn't need anyone either. A woman in general needs no man or woman to be happy or satisfied. It wasn't your fault it ended. Some things fall apart because hands get tired of holding it together. You cannot be upset or contribute your pain or anger towards someone who honestly needs more from themselves. You should be thankful you had time with them. Life is nothing more but collateral damage. You are going to get hurt eventually, more times than you will be comfortable with. You might as well hurt for the right reasons. Once a woman decides to leave any situation for herself, you will never be able to bring her back unless she wholeheartedly wishes to be. If she does return, fucking love her more than ever before. Tell her how proud of her you are. She chose to come back and include you. Choose her, infinitely.

I do not know if I am good enough for anyone. Days take me by the hand and lead me down a darkened path. There is no light to be found within me. There is no light to be kissed goodnight. I am troubled and plagued by nightmares. My soul wakes up before my body does. I have buried more than just secrets in my life. Some things can be wished upon forever, but it never brings them back. It only brings back the pain of missing them. I have had to say goodbye to more love than I have ever had in my life before. So far, I am doing my best. That is all you can really ask for when your heart will not go back inside your chest. When your hands cannot hold its fingers on a page. When your eyes are turned inside out. When nothing you do feels like it matters. But you do it all anyway. You do it, because you know at the end of the day, it is only you to come home to. You know you must take care of yourself. You must tend to your fields and gardens. You must tend to the rivers and oceans. You must tend to the temples, even if they resemble ruins these days. They still carry more promise than defeat.

I am always going to write about you. I do not know anything else. I do not want to forget your voice, so I write it in my words. You will always be safe in here; In my life, in my books, in my heart. I wasn't born to love anyone more than I do and have with you. I worry that I do not say it enough. That this is all something you do not want to remember. I hope you know I type gently in thought of you and with you in everything I do. I never want to put your progress in peril or what you want from your life in endangerment by me writing the way I do about you. The truth is, all I want you to know is that the love you gave me and the hope you kissed me with remains here, undoubtedly yours, forever. Even if we should never find one another again, I can still find you here. I know how important this new life of yours is. I know what it means for you. I know what it means for us. You are someone nobody could ever forget. Regardless of how many times one dies. You are the voice in my head. The incentive. The reason. Would I love a life with you? Of course, but the life you have now is more important than the one I could give you. Maybe one day we can ask for each other's name and begin from scratch.

With tears falling one by one, she told me, "I do not deserve you. You deserve so much more." I cannot help but love on her more when those doubts creep into that beautiful mind of hers. I gathered her emotions, energy, and body. I brought all of her as close to me as I could. Even with us snuggled on the couch, there is still too much space. There is still too much room for a doubt to be considered truth. We have always helped each other calm our breath and ease into a different kind of love. I told her, "I deserve you. If I deserve anything, it is you. I haven't had the easiest of times sleeping. It is difficult to do such a thing when your other half is awake. Though we are restless in a lot of ways, it is reassuring and comforting knowing you are awake when I am sleep. Distance still tells for us who we are, but there you will be and here I will stay. I am looking forward to holding all of the mess you say you are, so I can tell you how much I love your little lies about yourself. When I can clearly see you are the match for my soul.

You never liked the word, "No," in whatever case it was used. I have become the same way now. I will not let this be the end of what we both know is the rest of our lives. I will fight for you, for me, for us, until all that is left is a star named after our victory. One that will carry more than a love. It will dream of everything we did. Everything we became. Like us, it will birth a galaxy where all dreamers go when reality cannot fit into their fight. When it cannot stomp out what we burn for.

I would have married you the first day I saw you. I would have told you how much love it would take to make it work. I would have told you my heart holds yours not inside, but beside mine. I would have told you I was nervous and scared to hold your hand and sit next to you. A beauty like yours needs nothing or no one else with it for what and how it already is. I am nothing if not vulnerable and open. I am nothing if not a million ways to show someone how I love them. I am nothing if not yours. Never to beg. Never to steal. Never to be left. Your bad days are mine and I will do my best to make sure they stay away from that smile which made me marry someone who is too good for the bad in me.

Love may sound a little different coming out of my mouth these days, but each breath is still you. Every motion of my day is you. All of the words you still do not think belong to you, are yours. My life is nothing more than finding a proper balance of showing you and saving the rest for when I need to use my "ten." The magical thing about that sentence is that we only know what it means. I am still holding onto hope that you never forget what you meant to me. I turn around most days when someone speaks of a name. it is never mine, but I spin my head to see if it is you standing there. Love may sound differently to me now, but I still know how yours is the kind that never leaves anyone. No distance could ever keep it away or make it something I know it is not. A single breath of yours could keep me alive for the next fifty years. It has kept me alive thus far, so please, do not roll those pretty eyes at me in disbelief. It will only make me want you more.

There is this woman I know who has been tested by more than time and treated in such a way it makes me want to hunt down every man who has held her, only to drop the parts they couldn't handle. She has been kept together by keeping to herself when the night reaches for her heart and is struck with awe when they see the moon she has always been. Her fight is a rarity. Her love is timeless. Her eyes match her mood and can never be confused with being afraid. There is a part of her no one will ever be able to touch or probably contain. There is a part of who she is for her eyes only. Life knew what it was doing when it created her with fire and magic, with honey and stars, with attitude and grace. Only her body could withstand being this type of human, being this type of woman. Her books invite her softer side to be seen. The emotion of who she is. Not everyone is worthy of prompting such a thing, but her mind is not easily entertained. You must give effort. You must stimulate something more than what you are truly after. Death came to visit her when she was a child. If she can laugh at it and make it leave without saying a word, she isn't someone you can change. What you see is what you get. Good days, bad days, a beautiful mix of both. She is honesty and truth when you wish to only hear what you want. Once you become selective with her, she will go without telling you where. She has had those people in her life before. She will not make room for another. She is the final act.

Love never taught me to be normal or remain sane in my ways of wanting and craving whatever you offer to me. A body is only a playground if you kiss the stars just right. If you caress the moon gently while she sleeps in fractions and crescents. Love taught me to be wild, as she lays uncovered and begging for something to stay. Something to stick around between the heaven and hell she is placed between. There is nothing exact about us, and it is why we will always be able to contain one another when the shadows go looking for humans to play in their light; the hidden mirage of life and lust, dare and daring. We must never pretend to be any more than what we are. We will need to remove all human from our lives, because a soul is only as visible as the hand that can feel it. I will need to see you in this form. I will need you to see me, too. Whatever we touch and let into our reality, must be conceived by both of us. One where our devils can learn from our angels. One where both recognize it as an incurable ache for the sweetest fucking love ever made.

I consumed you. Maybe not enough to know every life you had lived before me, but enough to know I will never be able to rid you from my body. I go to stretch my arms and I feel your light. We submitted to love. It was the only time I had ever allowed myself to remain suspended in that state of mind. With you, I am an expression made from death and sacrifice. I am all the fucking terrible parts others hide away and lock up from anyone asking to see them. My scars were the first thing I showed you. It was the only way I knew if you would end up staying forever. Though that particular word has a slightly different meaning now, I know for a fact, a human whom you love with your entirety can never be unseen again. A billion faces could never change the way I see you. The way I feel you. A love close to the one like yours. I stay here, arms, mind, body, and spirit, stretched beyond their limits just to do it all over again. The chances I say I love you first again are high, but I will wait until your moon accepts my sun in a sky you are creating. One that you have earned and fought for.

I hope you never forget your beauty. One day, I will not be here to tell you. I hope it never goes unnoticed. I hope it never goes unloved. I hope nothing about you goes unappreciated, because you taught me the difference between want and need, between night and day. I hope you never know lonely in anything you do. Someone like you deserves to be told every fucking second how much you are love itself, its very core. Without you in this world, magic would be just another word to amaze any human looking for something they lost. When in fact, it is you who makes the word mean more than what one could ever find by someone else's defined definition.

I am tired. I am tired of guessing how you feel. I am tired of trying to win you back when I didn't want you to leave in the first place. I am tired of pretending to know who you are these days. We go months without talking and feelings shared. I tell myself it will be okay. I have no fucking idea if it ever will be. I am hoping you can forgive whomever you were to get back to me. I am not sure how much longer I can hold the sky above me, in hopes of your return to your rightful place next to me.

I will love you long after my heart erupts with flowers and my soul brings another star to the sky. There is no death for me when it comes to you and I. There are endless amounts of ways to show you how much I will love every piece of you in whatever life chooses us next. Your place amongst it will never be filled if you decide to leave for good. Should a day like that ever come, I will write about how you were the wildest creature I had ever known. One that was never able to settle for a home, but always ran barefoot into the sea.

She is more than love most days. I honestly have never met someone like her. I have stayed out underneath stars long enough to know when you are in the presence of an untamable force. It isn't about love. It is about connection. It is about being needed for the human she is, for the soul she bleeds out every night. She is hoping someone can run to her and put back what many have left alone and untouched for years. Not just physically touched, but adored, honored, fucking over the top emotional type of loving and touching. Where you pull her hair back just enough and play with it until the moon is moved. She longs for it all. A pure ache of madness. She is a force to be reckoned with. A force from where all beauty is born and backs down to no man. She is as sweet as the tea my grandmother makes, but will still stare you down long enough to make you know you are in the wrong. She doesn't need to say a goddamn thing. You either get it or you don't. I would sell all of my belongings just to be closer to her. Unexpected encounters have shaped my life, but this one, this woman, is too familiar in every sense of the breath. Our meeting had been planned. She can be the devil's hand, but I would still hold it and follow her clear off the fucking map.

\I just want to make you feel what I do. Not by pressuring you or telling you, but living out the truth behind it. I can only be here with you if you want what I am offering. If you do, I will take down the stars for you. I will bring you every moon that created you. My love is not for everyone, but I do hope it is something you can live with. I do hope it is something you will need, day in and day out, just as much as I need yours.

I always knew I was going to need you more than you needed me. But it didn't stop me from loving you and giving you all I had left. That's what you do when love is the only fucking thing you are after. That's what you do when love is all you can say when trying to get words out of a mouth that had been shut and locked up because one time in your life, love was nothing more than dead flowers and lonely nights. You brought it all back to life. You made lonely forget I existed. Even if you are gone for good, you made love come back to me and gave goodbye a new name. When goodbye becomes you, the only thing left to do, is to resist the temptation of remaining alone and broken, afraid of ever opening your chest up for someone else. We were damned long before the curse was handed to us. We were born alone, but it is the journey of finding someone to be alone with that will keep me upright and joyful.

No matter how much it fucking hurts, you cannot stay where you think you are needed. You must know without any hesitation that you are worthy of something better than second guessing. You must feel it in your goddamn soul. If you do not feel it there, leave and never look back. Eventually, you will find someone running in the same direction as you and you will be able to slow down long enough to feel something besides doubt creeping up behind you. When it is real, love will only ask you to stay. It is there you will find what others before never could offer. It is there any and all damaged humans will rejoice with life in their eyes. It is there your mistakes and failures will forgive you.

I knew I could not always write about love. Death and I know each other too well. We are too close to ever have love stay forever. Certain bonds you make, keep you from ever having what you feel as though is yours to have always. So tonight, when you sleep, just know I wish I could love you as much as the devil loves me. Just know I tried to love you more than you had ever been before. My attempts were valid, but you never looked to me for validation. I saw goodbye in your eyes long before he came back into your life. I simply chose to believe I was who you needed, when it was never me to begin with.

I always thought I would be the first to leave. I guess that's why it hurts so fucking much. You never truly comprehend the impact of the rest of your life leaving you before your soul leaves your own body. I know we met for a reason, and for that alone, I am thankful for our encounter. I needed it. I needed you in this life. For however long it ended up being, it was a singular part of my life I will look back on one day and smile at, knowing how goodbye isn't always the end of a love story. Chapters close so new ones can begin. It is the oldest tale of existence. Leave the pages blank until you are ready to draw blood from your own stories to create the next one.

There are a lot of things going through my mind. I am wondering if two years ago was the last time our arms will ever embrace the other. If all we have done will be past tense without it ever changing into present day. If you will still think of me during the times you are lonely or if you have already found someone to replace me and my body. I just want more time to look at you in the eyes and kiss your lips as hard as I can and leave the imprint of my soul on yours. I told you lonely would never know your name. I do not want it to know mine either. Maybe after the earth comes back around again, everything will be okay. There is a change in you, as if you already know something I do not. If you can get over me this quickly, where do I stand when there is no room for my body? I will still hope that my intuition isn't always right, especially when it comes to you. But I can feel your absence, as if it was the moment before we knew each other existed. The commonality of all strangers and former lovers.

I still wonder what life could have been for us. I will never forget the first time I saw your picture and what it did to me. I wanted you before we even spoke a single word to one another. I wanted you before I knew anything about what made you happy. We had met before. We had loved a million years ago. Maybe one day we can try again. Souls never forget the humans they eventually become.

I could have done without this heartache. I am too fucking old to hate anyone these days or to feel something I did not deserve. Protect yourself at all costs. Love should never fucking destroy who you are. It should never feel like a casket closing or shoveled dirt into your mouth and eyes. You destroyed me. I hope you never read this if I am being honest. I do not wish to give you any more room in my books for the ache that you have given me. I do not wish to give you any more space in my life's work that you once helped me create. I do not wish to forget about you or keep you from seeing my life. I want you to see how happy I can be and will be with the love awaiting me down the line. Somewhere in that space alone, I will tie off what I can and hang what's left of you for my demons to play with when I am finally removed from you.

We are still learning how to be in love while being together. It is a trying time to say the least, but if love is what you want, you will dig until you get underneath the bones of it all. You will do all you can to provide yourself a rightful opportunity for it to outlast whatever doubt you have floating around in your head.

Pictures tend to stay the same until the humans inside of them become less of a moment and more of a forgotten memory. Where smiles are frozen, but feelings become full of hatred, with an expressionless face. Now I know why you had your reasons to never take any with me. One less thing for you to have to destroy in the end. One last thing to hide in the box and darkness where you kept me. I thought I was protecting you, but you were killing me.

Life is going to be fucking hell for you the next few months, but I know you will make it. I know the blood inside of you. I know the love inside you. There was never any quit within you. A beautiful fight was given to you by the gods, cosmos, and the stars before you. I am happy for you, even if at times I am cold with you. It will take me some time to forget how to love you and be merely a friend. I wouldn't have made it out alive with the life I was leading if you had not given me what you did. Now, it is my turn to give you a goodbye, but not the forever kind. Now, it is my turn to give you what you are asking of me.

You will constantly be on my mind as I go on without you. My heart has been trying to break through my ribs to get to you. To say it hasn't been painful would be a fucking understatement. It is difficult finding a breath when your lungs hold my air. I told you before, what is mine, is yours. I am a newborn again, with hands and feet dangling at the edge of infancy. I am a new man, with eyes and speech still trying to catch up to everything I have been feeling.

I have learned if you want to live a good life, you must overcome the rules. You must overcome the expectations. You must break at least one dream over a star to ignite a particular purpose. After it is done, everything you need becomes a meaning for you, a dedicated approach to freedom. It will become a necessary love, which is the only truth in our lifetime worth believing in.

I don't need to see how you smile at him, knowing he will never be able to see how I once smiled at you. I hope he treats you well and with safe hands. I will not say I hope he treats you better than I did, because I gave you more than I had ever given to anyone in my entire life. Sometimes, you cannot please someone just by giving, and that is what happened between us. You grew tired of my love when your love would have always been enough for me.

You said you would never do what she did to me, but you lied. You fucking became her. You left me. I hope whomever you end up with does the same to you when you least expect it. I hope it hurts like I am hurting now. I hope it sticks with you forever like a mighty thorn in your side. As badly as we never want to inflict pain onto those we love, we all eventually become those we hate in the end.

It all makes sense now. You used me to have someone there you needed during this entire time you were trying to free and find yourself. You needed someone to tell you all of those fucking things you could never believe yourself so you could feel better about who you were and what we were doing. Now that it is over with you two, you do not need me anymore, because I helped you get to this point. Fuck me right? Love is a wild thing when it is disguised as a devil and being played by a woman. You once told me I would never have to worry about him, but I knew in my bones I did and would eventually lose out to you leaving me for his love. I have learned just how much I take pleasure in torturing myself when it comes to love and its tragedies.

She was a little bit chaotic, even for herself at times. It was a fire within her that kept her balanced and able to walk amongst a field of wildflowers without losing her sense of adventure. There are stories that will be told about who she was, long after all of this is over. It is the legend she became that haunts those who never believed in her, when all she wanted was love and to be loved.

And I will keep going about my day loving you all I can. It was once my favorite part of the day I had created with you. I will keep loving you more each time I breathe in a sunrise and exhale a sunset. I have fallen in love with more ghosts than humans as of late, but it is what keeps my insanity from overtaking my entire life.

I have loved you with every fucking part of my existence. Now, I must learn how to look at the sky and forget the moon is there. Finding my way now is what my life has become. I will still share my secrets, but this time, I will not be able to share my love. One day I will again, just not at this present moment. Each step takes me further away from you. Distance has become my adventure.

As much as my heart can hold, I still love you. As much as my bones can grow, there will always be room for you. Humans never forget those who place a light inside of its home. They never forget those who helped them out of a thousand graves they dug by themselves to keep the world away from every part of their life.

I know it won't be easy, but please, sweet woman, remind me of you. Remind me why you are here. Remind me how love never leaves soulmates. Remind of how your hands created the earth underneath my feet and the fire that speaks your name when the flames exude out of me. Remind me. Remind me. Remind me of you.

That is the thing about moving on or at least trying to; some humans become your limbs and others become your soul. Which if you are brave enough to leave it all behind, may the missing pieces of who you are, find you again when you are ready for an ultimate change. Some things just aren't made for goodbye. I am no different. My body shakes and I cannot even get the fucking word out of my mouth. I will never say it, because you know how endearing my stubbornness is. But I will give you space so you can do what you need to. I will be here. Whether in words or light, if you need me, you will find me.

There will be you and everything we once were. Those are the moments I will hold onto most throughout my life. You were always light years away from me, but I never felt as close to you as I did that day laying with you in the mess we made. Those moments taught me how to love myself. Those moments taught me how to love again. They brought me trust, peace, and the ability to have control over my life. In our time together, we can only hope for someone to lead us to ourselves, after being lost amongst the brokenness of who we were. You will be my favorite memory and my endless heartache once you are walking away from me.

It doesn't hurt that you left. It is the fact I gave you my best when you said it would always be enough. But you still let go of us. That kind of pain puts bodies into the ground and souls lost without a cause to live for. That kind of pain keeps bleeding and slaps a thousand smiles off of your face. We all have our reasons. I just hope the next one you find, you do not tell him what you told me. No one else needs to know this hurt. No one else needs to know how it looks from six feet below the earth, looking up for someone to stop throwing in the dirt.

I guess it is time I stop writing about you. I know it won't bring you back to me. I know it is just me talking to myself at this point. I know you are gone for good, regardless of what you say. When you go from loving someone for years and telling them every random thing about your life, to zero contact without any explanation, nothing else needs to be said or discussed. Maybe one day I will be able to not think of you while I write. Maybe one day I can finally find the right words that I obviously never got around to telling you. I can only hope the next person gives you more. I can only hope the next person makes you happy. I can only hope that this type of goodbye never happens to me again.

A goodbye came in the form of you leaving without saying a goddamn thing to me other than, "I will always be here." It is hard to see you here, knowing you are finally gone. Five years of plans. Five years of patience. Five fucking years of us. I type with anger and frustration. I type with some hope on the ends of my fingertips that by the time I am done writing this, you will be back. But I am going to keep this short, just as you did with your silence towards my questions. To the days and years we could have had together, I will make sure to spend them with myself first, before I go back into love. No one deserves this version of me. It kills me to think someone gets the version of you where you are okay with everything. I will not wish you good luck with anything, because it was luck that brought me you. I have none left to give. You were it.

I remember I would write you handwritten notes for you to wake up to. Back when everything was simpler. Back when you slept and thought of me. Back when I would stay up with you for hours so you wouldn't be alone. I still have them and I am unsure of what will become of them. I do know what I will do with my life. Maybe not all of it, but I have an honest idea as to where I am heading after all of this pain subsides. The last one before you damn near killed me. I guess you just wanted to see how deep you could push the blade in before I screamed mercy. You have left your mark on my life. I remember I almost tried to leave a few times when we first started this, because of the guy you are now with. You never had to tell me I was wrong or right about him. I always knew, but I was trusting you with my life, while you were trusting yourself with the prepared goodbye you had ready for me. You gave up long before you uttered the words. I felt the shift last November. I could tell something had happened. I understand it, because you were fighting for your own freedom at that time. But it all comes down to not giving up on those you love and whom love you back; relationships, friends, or family. If there is love present, it is always worth it. I wish I had been worth more than wasted time to you.

You left me without saying anything. You cut off all communication. You ghosted everything we were or would ever hope to become. I think I saw this coming. I had doubts in the beginning when someone else popped back into your life, but you told me not to worry about it. You fucking lied straight to me face and rotted the inside of my soul with your lies. You were skeptical of it all back then, but you chose me, or so I thought. When life became what it is for you now, you stopped needing me the way I needed you. Was it love? I ask myself a few times a day if it was really something poets can bring to life. For me, it was love. For you, I guess it was some fucking game you got tired of playing when your past showed up. It was a way for you to forget about the life you were leading. I gave you an out, an escape. I gave you a way out of feeling nothing, to feeling everything you had been missing. I had no backup plan, nobody else who could ever take your place. I felt it then and I should have left before these five years had passed. We did have our moments though. We had a lot to fight for, but your fight was never made for us when shit got difficult. It isn't in you. It isn't who you are. You need security. You need stability. I am the most random and chaotic human in the world more times than not. Next time, do not fuck with a heart that is true to your own just because you are alone. Do not fuck with one that would do anything to keep yours safe. Whomever you find to take the place of me, you deserve each other. We all get what we fight for. You never deserved me in the first place. You won't ever find my fight in someone else.

Now I can be in a relationship where I do not have to hide you. Where I do not have hide our love. Where I do not have to hold back what I feel and what I want. Being free in love will now be my choosing. Now more secrets. No more deceit. Now it is just me and the world; ever so empty. ever so full.

If you should ever go lonely, may it be for a better place, a more pronounced feeling, an ocean of your own love. A hummed hallelujah will enter the universe. There you will find your reasons. There you will find your gold. It is all waiting for you to let go of what you're currently holding onto that is holding you back.

I am asking why it happened when this is already enough to kill someone. In all seriousness, I sincerely hope I never find out why you did this to me and how long it was going on behind my back. It is the gunshot to the head no one sees coming. It is the bullet fired from close range. Please, keep it all holstered for me. My death will not come from a coward.

I had a dream about you the other night. You were with him on the beach. It was a dream you once told me you had of him before we began talking and became what we did. I had the invitation in my hand. I looked at it, then looked up to see you staring back at me. I shook my head and you nodded yours. I turned away and threw the invitation into the sea. You are the one wish I hope never comes back to me.

I am not as strong as I once told you I was. I cannot keep the entire world above my head and still hold onto you. I thought I would be the one who told you, "I do." The thing that hurts me the most is that I honestly loved you and you still fucking left me with my heart cut out of my goddamn body. I must let you go now. I must let it all be known how to survive the inevitable. I must let you go if I am ever to hold anyone else who actually wants to be in my arms. It isn't easy living with a broken soul, but I am trying.

She's kissing me like she means it. As if I am the only one her lips were meant for. To me, she is perfect, but she has a hard time believing it. I once saw what we could be when I looked into her eyes. I now see us through my own, well beyond the horizon that kept us apart. I never want to be without her. A heart like mine needs a soul like hers. She tried to save me once, but it was me trying to keep her safe all this time. I knew from the moment of learning her name, it would be the last thing I would ever say that could keep me from my own insanity. I am no longer lonesome or afraid. I am a writer, living in a book about the love she gave to me.

This is the sound of a broken heart healing. These are the words you will never hear me say. I may still love you, but I will never trust you or need you in the way I used to. Your grave is full now of everyone you have buried along the way of uncovering yourself. My anger towards you is nothing more than resentment, a true disappointment of what and who you turned out to be.

Goodbye, moon.

Your light will be kept safe. Your gentle love will be remembered. I know you will find a new sky to shine in. I know they will be thankful for it just as I was. Goodnight, sweet wonder.

This is the ending of what was us. This is final page I will ever truly dedicate to you. These are the roses. This is the eulogy spoken by our souls. This is where something will rise again to find life. What we have buried here will only be as beautiful as the life we create for ourselves moving forward without each other. I have given you words and kept your name safe from anyone knowing who you were when I wrote. My sentences were your safety. The only thing that will change is how far away you are from me. You are not allowed to stay. Our ending was much like our beginning; unexpected and unsure. It seems appropriate and honorary to go out the same.

There is a love out there for us. It takes blood, dreams, and dying a little bit each day. It takes us to the very edge of who we are, then brings us back whole, ripped apart, and cleansed. We are the chosen ones for this life and everything it gives and takes away from us. We are the children of light and darkness. We are the lovers of the broken and numb. We give anything we can, because we know how it feels to go without a shoulder to lean on or a backbone to hide behind. The love we are after, is the purpose of life. Where we go, no one else has ever been before. It is what makes this place as beautiful and tragic as it is for some of us. But we will be victorious. We will know what love is and can be for us, for those willing to bring the moon down before it goes unloved.

I have so much love to give and nowhere to put it, no one to give it to. It seems as though most days I am only wearing caution tape around my entire body and looking for excuses as to why I do. My soul is bursting at its seams for something greater than what I have had and what always leaves. Maybe I am meant to walk around with nothing more than my lonely showing, while seeing everyone else pass me with love slapped on their faces. Maybe my curse is to know of love, to see love, to be ever so fucking close to it, without it ever knowing I exist, without it ever asking how I am and what kind of pain I live with. I feel like an idiot even thinking that way, because I know how bad others have it. I know there is so much evil out there, taking names and hearts each day. I do not feel sorry for myself, though I have doubt I will ever find someone who is ready. Someone who is ready to be loved in such a way that it would make the moon blush. I look at you now, still knowing your name and a little about who you are, I feel as though it is all you will ever be to me. Someone who is too human for me to give another heart to. Someone who is content with what they already have. Someone who is still trying to figure out their own life. I know I am the same way, but goddamn, there are days when I want to be wrapped in you and tell you how you give my heart its name. How you found a broken man who knew only pain before your hands made magic out of my ruins. I am going to give you space, because one time, someone gave me the same. It turned out we weren't meant for each other. This time, I believe there is more to gain than ending up without you. You are the thunder before the rain. You are the few seconds of pause before the lightning. You are the storm I have waited my whole life to chase. But for now, you are a few clouds in the distance, with just enough sun shining through to give me hope.

I know things won't ever be the same. It kills me to say it, even more so to believe myself when I hear me speak it. But you are over me, while I am pretending you still care about my life. It is an admirable job you are doing. Giving me just enough of you to keep me around. I am playing into your hands. When I get to your state, I will know for sure if I can move on like you have, like you have so easily done without caring how deep you cut into my bones. I wonder if you ever cared how many times you broke me down in the months since you had left. I know I need to let go, but there has always been something about me that loves pain, agony, self-inflicted brutality. I cannot escape the addiction it gives me. I cannot escape you. At least not yet, but even my own reasons fall at the earth's edge if pushed far enough. I am tired of writing to your ghost. I am tired of portraying you as some real thing in my life, when you are no more a reality than love marrying chaos because it, too, thrives off of brokenness. Where one person sees saving, another sees an opportunity to do something good for a change. It is about time I change it all and hand back what is left of me to the universe that gave me another chance to live. Sometimes I confuse life and love and interchange them, but they are only interchangeable when given to the right person. When they are responsible. When they are never careless to someone caring. I am out of chances to give you, but a muse never dies. You will live long after the words aren't about you. One day, you will see how much I really did love you, when the one you love next is incapable of loving you more than my words ever showed you.

Love was a new feeling with you. I had said it before you and felt something for someone. I had felt truth somewhere in the voice I used to speak with. When I said it to you, I felt the world shake and the universe tremble. My hands pointed directly to who you were. There is still that feeling with you. My hands simply hang at my side now. My voice refuses to utter a single letter of your name.

I have never known anyone like you and that is why it is so damn hard moving on from you. Some humans make too much sense to you for them to be an afterthought. Something that becomes past tense, but still present in an incalculable way. They are a radical change in appearance of soul. A new way to eat, sleep, and breathe. A mending of all nightmares and misfortune. It wouldn't have mattered if it was a single day or a lifetime replayed over and over again. You would still matter to me the same. You would still be the dew on a fresh day. The first sip of coffee after running down your demons from the night before. A single breath of air escaping an ocean's wave. The flight of a butterfly to a flower it loved more than its reason for flying. The first kiss you will feel when you are eighty and holding hands to keep her close. The day before a celebration to celebrate who she is before anyone can speak about her. You would still matter to me, darling. At times, I feel pathetic and delusional for writing to you and about you since we barely talk anymore. But I think this is what you are supposed to do when love becomes every reason to give a little more than you should. When love finds you, you are struck a million times with the softest and most tender of ways in a heart you swore your life on you would never give again. Last time we spoke, your voice sounded different. It happens when time passes without contact. In my head, I can still hear you the same as I did when I first called you that night when you told me not to. You told me recently how you felt your world crumble around you. It pains me to know that, but if you were me watching my world crumble, you would understand how I feel right now. It is one thing watching your own life fall apart before your eyes, but when you see both go, all of it crushes you. All of it sits on your chest, waiting on you to give up hope. As much as I want to, I fucking cannot. It doesn't make me weak to say it. In life, we only get a few chances to love and fight. We only get a few tries at saying everything we mean. Writing will always be my purpose. Writing about you will be my story. At least I know where you will be. At least I know how to write a meaningful goodbye.

If you feel me get up in the middle of the night, keep resting your eyes, sweet one. It is just my mind. It is just my heart. It is just my soul. It is just me walking to my typewriter to express what I cannot tell you while you sleep. Some days, I know I love you more than you love me. Please do not get upset when I say that. I do not expect anyone to ever give me my love in return. That is not life. That is not what love is to me. Some days, I know you have to be more distant, just as I have to. My closeness to you is not an exact measurement, rather a feeling of connected atoms, sunsets, sunrises, and dying stars, all trying to breathe again. I keep looking over my shoulder to see if this typing is making you walk near me. Sometimes, you cannot punch the keys hard enough or soft enough. Maybe there is a happy medium I am missing. Maybe I am just missing you too fucking much. I am trying to be quiet, but you know my heart too well to know I lack passion. Some days, I catch myself thinking how differently it all would have been if I had just let you go back then. If I had just given into my intuition and let go of us. If I had just told you sooner about what I wanted us to be. Love knew you and I long before our lives knew each other. It knew what it was doing, because I had never met anyone who made me get up in the middle of the night to write something for them to read in the morning. Never had I met someone who I knew could hold my attention and laughter quite like you did. During the noiseless moments, I hear your laugh. It still gives me chills and makes my smile mean more than the curves it makes around my cheeks. Maybe when all of this is over, I can see you again. Maybe you can be around me like before. After this, I will return to a bed that used to keep us both made and satisfied. In my mind, you are still there. Call me crazy, call me anything you would like. Love makes us all a bit mad. If I have to go through life seeing you everywhere, I am here for it. I did not know my name until I knew yours.

There will be a time for love. There will be a time to leave. There will be a time to stay, to hold. There will be humans along the way who will give your life a new definition, a new route. There will be a time to cry, to purge. There will be humans who will help you along your way to do just that. Sometimes for the better. Other times for reasons unknown until a few long years down the road. There will be an ache within you for each one. There will be words left unsaid, because saying anything means the end to something you never knew could die. There will be nights when a bed cannot make you rest or keep you laying down. There will be mornings you wish could stay fresh with tender light a bit longer for your soul to taste, so you can drink in what the universe left behind for it to loosen up the stars within its throat. There will be boredom instead of wildness. Do not wish for anything more than what you have. One day, it, too, will be gone. There will come a day when you will have to decide for yourself what is more important between love for self and love for another. I hope there is no hesitation. I hope there is no regret. I hope the only pause given is when you go to hold whichever one you decide on. A human can only take so much loss until they become the loss. Until whatever their life consisted of, is now a backstory to a life who has to explain why this happened and why this didn't happen. Leaving this life, you have now, for something you deem as better, takes courage, fight, and a resisting urge to fall back into what you once believed to be who you were. The funny thing is, you may be that person to only yourself. No one might have seen that before, but you never forget what pain looks like in the middle of the night, you never forget how it feels to crawl out of your skin to escape what you are dealing with within. I am a billion people inside of a body. I am a million emotions starving for truth. I am one word away from being myself. The thing is, I have basically grown into everyone I have encountered. I am, you. We are, each other. All of these years, I have been pronouncing the word all wrong. Your name sounds different today. Your voice has gone underground, but it still shakes me to the core of who it is I am without you.

There are still things I hope to do with you. Sitting at a table with you across from me. Getting up to sit beside you, because there is still too much distance. Walking with you down the sidewalk, not having to hold your hand, but still reaching for it to feel your skip, your mood. Watching a sunset, whilst having my coffee and you with your tea. I am almost one hundred percent certain we would not catch many sunrises since you are not a morning person, but I would bring you the picture I took of it so you could see how you shine. It takes a lot of energy and love to light up an entire sky. I can go without touching you, kissing you, telling you, I love you, if that makes it easier for you. The devil may know my name, but when you say it, my soul goes up in flames. I can sit with you, talk to you, and just watch you breathe. I can do all of it without having to jeopardize the progress you have made, if you can give me five minutes, I will be able to write you a poem every day until your body becomes a part of the earth. You are still my best friend. If you should ever go before I do, I will bury each one into the ground for you to feel how much of you is still walking this place, when all it took was five minutes to memorize a moon not from this planet.

Most days, it is hard for me to hear the truth and even more so to tell it. I lay my face next to your breath and I feel a million flowers birthing from your smile. The sweet luscious flavor of forgiveness leaves the room. Every fear dies. Every mistake taken off its cross. Truth bleeds and tonight I am drained. I am trying to remember how conviction works when you are not here. I am trying to remember if my words have ever spoken to anyone besides you. My flesh next to yours. My ache next to your strength. My imperfections next to your beauty. None of it ever made sense to me. I never did understand the moon. I hope I never need to. She is, because she wishes to be. You are, because she has always been a replica, a second-hand attempt at becoming you. But there is victory in trying. There is victory which never marches, but walks beside love. My body next to yours, I trace one of your fingertips. To the nail, to the cuticle, to the shade of black which colors the tips. I am in awe of how much power there is when touch is present. I am in awe of how much relevance there is in movement against another immovable object. I lay my life down next to yours and it adds another five here and another ten there. As long as my own hands never stop working, I will type for you and about you. For if they should be mangled by life, I will speak to you the words and you can type for me if you wish. My words and baby blue typewriter have always loved you more. I never gave her a name, which is why some days she hates me. Though in reality, I did name her, but some things are better to be left alone until reason calls for it to surface and touch life. Until then, my life is writing your name as a different word each time.

There is so much to be said about the way a woman can love you well beyond what you deserve. She gives me hope that possibly nothing else exists and the world really does care about its humans. During the moments of complete nothingness, she will always fucking matter. Her voice and moans will forever be given a reply of mutual satisfaction.

I will remain adrift with a soul made from sin in the ashes of my early death, when I was a child seeing the life lose its breath before me. The innocence brings you back to a place which celebrates indifference and challenges hierarchy of judgment. We have replaced truth with lies just to feel better. We have given away all of the good we had, to have it good enough for now. Birds fly south not only to escape winter, but to bring out a balance of old and young. To create a new home and enabling its youth to fly or fail depending on the exhale of a breeze. I, too, will be made by mountains or turned into the grains of sand escaping my hands as I call out your name one last time. There is a time for death, but not now, not without being next to you for a lifetime, living and loving everything we create.

Maybe I cannot give you what you need at this point in your life, but if you are willing to live with me in the unknown for a little while longer, maybe we can make it out of here together. Maybe we can make it with a promise only to love as long as our lungs fill with the breath of each star watching us grow towards the moon above us. My hopes of reaching you will never cease.

It is raining here today. Not a common thing for this area, but it is a reminder to be still in life at times. It is not always about running the tread off of your soul. It is about taking root in the earth below you. You must water each leaf of it. You must water every emotion, feeling, and ache. Without the love of change, we would stop being human. Consistency depends on your definition of the word. I can only hope success greets your accomplishments the same way the sun embraces our darkness. Once it goes behind our eyes, the sun may never rise again.

My lungs are tired from holding in second guesses and unspoken words. Just like with anything on its last legs, we will need to find a quiet place to rest our hunger, our pain, our defeats. We are strangers to organs putting in overtime, when they deserve lovely sighs and motionless punctuations. We are parents long before the kids announce us as such. Our first responsibility means keeping alive what keeps us alive. We are born with that burden, with that beautiful proclamation of giving more than what we have.

Living to feel soul. Wandering to feel life. Loving to feel earthly. Listening to feel each step beside you. Hopelessly becoming less bounded by burdens and more freely attached to the water inside of me. When you are thirsty, my body will unconditionally give you what it is you are after. It knows only survival when it comes to this life and a love not of my own.

I am at a crossroads in my life with love. It is such a waiting game to play. It is such a slow death to be given. Not knowing when or if they will ever be ready. Not knowing if you deserve more than having your eyes seeing something that is not fucking there. The only time we waste, is the time spent unsure of our decisions. That is why they are called what they are. I do not know if the answers will gradually visit me or if they will kill me in my sleep with silence. All I am sure of, is this place is undefeated when it comes to doubt and uncertainty. Hopefully they both do not take you behind the eyes of a blinded soul, engulfed by an incurable sense of needing and giving affection. Sometimes, love is only make-believe, but I swear to whatever god reigns over this ball of misfits and excuses for life, I believe in something more for me, for you, for us, than the emptiness others give us when we drain our bodies to fill theirs with what we want in return.

There is too much air in these lungs to be wasted on arguing with you about what love is and what it is not. If my soul feels anything, it is artful and real. We only decide if it is meant to be shared with someone else. Other than that, let us just be our best versions of the magic needed to give into the temptation of it all.

Allow love to be not only everything you need, but a singular presence in your life. It all begins when the lies end. Until then, we are floating along this life, with merely a breeze keeping us from falling over or flying.

I am still getting used to being someone your heart used to ask about. I am sure it is better this way. I am sure you are happier. Pictures say a lot about a human's life. Those spots where no one else is looking. Those grins no one else sees. I hope you still save a few of those for yourself. I hope the ring he gives you doesn't mirror the one I would have given you. I hope your vows have nothing to do with what we talked about. I hope you never think of me again, because I had thought about the day when we would be together long enough for a few lifetimes to encapsulate who we were. I am still getting used to seeing images of me without you, but I still grin and laugh at what we had. It was universally accepted and that is how I know it will work out for you both. You found it again, and that makes me even happier for you. One day, I will smile at someone else and not have to think about the days where I thought I was dying without you.

Maybe I cannot love you the way I want to now, but it will not keep my soul from trying to protect yours. It will not stop me from sending the sun to check on you. It will not keep me from writing a million pages as to why we will work and how my crazy needs yours. A half-soul will always be more capable of defeating the odds for its other half. The only thing distance or timing does to it, is make the roots become a system of never-ending feelings being expressed through actions. Some days I wonder if my love was something you craved or if they were a toy you would use to make yourself the only one who was happy when we both found a way to say goodnight.

Love limps past me like an animal who injured their legs while running after its favorite toy. Slowly, it fades and is gone forever. There are no promises any of us could ever make that would not be hindered in some way by a love gone astray. We can only hope to come back to someone who was not the one who hurt us to begin with. We must grow towards and after good company whose intentions on being upfront about their own history of hurting or being hurt.

You are the greatest expression of anything my mind plants and then becomes. The growing of seasons become endless. If there ever were to be another bloom fall from my face, it is only a weep of purity existing within the very particles of earth and universe that make you whole. When the sun finally comes to rest, it is not from shining or shedding its light. It is simply choosing to be closer to you the same way my head and heart react when the night summons us to be closer. Gardens grow from my fingers, and as the rose begins to smile, my life makes sense again. Everything is just another expression, because all of them are for you and about you.

I am trying my best not to smother you, while allowing there to be a healthy space for you. I am trying my best, because all I want to do if I am being honest, is talk to you every fucking second I am awake. I do not want you to think I am not interested in you or what you have to say or the life you are living. We all over-think when it comes to caring about someone you hope is never removed from your journey. Especially the ones who bring a sense of understanding of who you are. They make you believe in all things beautiful. They make you realize it can be yours, too. Sometimes, they make it to where you cannot go a minute without thinking about them and that is the most precious gift. From the way our sun kisses the sky, all the way to our moon collecting secrets, this view is better when I am looking at it all with you. I am trying not to overdo it, but I overdo everything when it comes to the love I have to give to you.

We are all going to die from something, so please, my darling, allow me to love you until I am born again into your life. There is only so much you can do with an ache like this, but I have a feeling you know how it is to miss someone you have yet to meet. I know nothing else about this world, except when the days seem to hurt more than the distance covering the absence of you from me and everything living and breathing inside of this old soul of mine.

I do not know how to let go. These hands only know how to keep what was never meant for them. They have bled from picking up broken glass from the box my heart was kept in. They have calloused over with stone and concrete, hoping they would never become soft again for a face to touch. They have tattoos on them to keep away those who find it to be a sin to mark your body. They have scars on them from holding up the sun for those who never could sleep at night. Each finger is stained with a color and feature of where the pain came from by pointing at others. They are cursed to direct life when all life is dead, when all life is gone from sight. Long after the love has left. Long after the flower has been given and stepped on. I am nothing more than petals at this stage of my cycle, but I still hold onto a chance of hope by allowing the wind to fly me, the sky to guide me, and the rains to water what is left of a reason to stay.

I cannot change my appearance. I am this way for a reason. I will always be this way, just with more wrinkles, less hair, droopy skin, and dentures at some point. I will keep dying just to live a single marked or unmarked day with you. If it never happens, I hope you remember me as I am now. I hope you can picture me as an older man, telling stories of how we met and how I knew I loved you before I knew your name. Some people fall in love with faces. Some people fall in love with a laugh. Some people fall in love with security. If I am to be in love, may it be with a soul that touched mine and made me forget what being human meant, because to me, it is only about loving each breath that comes out of my mouth since our star exploded all those lifetimes ago.

I love knowing you will be there when I get up. I love looking at my phone when your name pops up. I turn into a goddamn kid who was just invited to his own planetarium and is never asked to leave. I love being able to see it all with you; the fire, water, earth, all possible outcomes. There is a truth about lips speaking soulish secrets. When bodies are devoured by bravery tending to a call for no retreat. I am nervous to meet you, because your beauty has never been present in my life. If I start to shake or fumble my words, just know it is me being honest.

No one quite gets her and that is the point. She does what she wants without a single attempt to look for your opinion on her life. She smiles though, and when she does, those tiny fucking cracks you have are filled with her magic. She is not always happy-go-lucky, but you could never tell by the love she has for all things full of soul, the attitude of kings and queens. A little recklessness never got in her way of success. Self-made is her status, even when the day engulfs her dreams and spits them back out at her, she makes art with it all. Between finding who she is and who she was, there are not many with the capability of moving mountains and overcoming storms to unearth sweet relief and gold in the form of inner peace and acceptance for her journey. Each day is a way of becoming wilder than before, but it is who she is; wings, horns, halo, and all.

I see you beyond the colors on your face you so elegantly wear. I see the fresh skin as pure as flowers beneath the sun. I see a woman who is still in search of something and doing it all with such a love, the world around you becomes a kind and forgiving place. I see a smile mixed with a laugh that changes how a universe is made. There is only chaos if we choose to become it. There is only love if we choose to share it. There is only hope if our lungs believe it. I see you, the sweetest soul to have ever walked into my life. I see you, magic, stars, and a collection of unfulfilled promises, configured to be something so remarkable, it makes me want to give you a million kisses and give thanks for staying as long as you have. Maybe tomorrow I can find a better way to hold you and tell you all of this again in a more endless way.

Life will not always make sense. Sometimes, humans come into your life to fuck it all up, but even with that comes growth; spiritually, mentally, and emotionally. They show you where you are still healing and where your focus needs to be in your life. Do not fall back into believing everyone is out to get you. Your strength lies within the actions that follow. Pick yourself up, wipe off the blood or paint it on the walls and leave it there as a reminder when you walk past it. You will know who the fuck you are and what you are in need of in your own life. Motivational speakers and self-help books will only get you so far until you become your own for the life you want.

I let you in and you collapsed all I had built. You made me believe in your lies. All you wanted from me was not to feel alone. All you wanted was to fuck over someone else to make yourself feel better about going back to the guy who broke you more than anyone should ever be. You made me believe I could be open with you and get it back in return. You are just another pretty little thing, a balancing act of deceit and fraudulence, pretending to love yourself. You can go back to him. You just wanted to shed your losses and allow someone who has words you love to read. But if you only knew what I would have done for you. I hope it fucking hurts the next time he fucks you over. It is going to happen. Men love to feed off of women who are happy to hold the devil, if it means they get to keep the precious gifts he gives. To think, I thought you had spine, when you only used mine to find protection behind. Go now with the night and I will make sure the moon never remembers your name. I will make sure her shine never gets confused with yours.

Longing to be loved is unlike anything you will ever experience. The pain is unbearable. The anguish torments your demons. The empty pit where all your hope goes to die. The smoldering ashes of who you thought you were will lie there forever. The tired eyes that beg for relief, but it never comes. It is an endless flood that fills your insides with hopelessness. Your skin begins to peel back. Deserts remain a wasteland for backpackers looking for a way home. I know nothing else in this life. I am love, but still it evades me like a fallen bird whose wings have failed him since the accident. It will continue falling until it lands to a death only to be embraced by the finality of suffering. Truth feels better when it is spoken out loud.

She has always been the poetry and soul of it all. She is a quiet beautiful, but thunderously in love with words and the fall. She is pure Americana, a tender display of vintage for eyes that need to see how life should be lived. A kiss to the stars and she is off again to break the hearts of those who will attempt to redirect her path.

I am still madly in love with my wild and solitude. I am a beastly creature in search of a warm and forgiving light. It was once your hand that gave me release. Now it is your hand taking my heart out of me and doing what you do best with things that are not yours.

I wanted it to be you. Now you are just another human with a piece of me. Too many these days are walking around with who I used to be. I thank them for taking that man away. He was never going to be any good for you. He was just trying to help and probably fucked it up somewhere after saying hello and buying you things to make you happy. Lessons visit us all the time. Unless you put forth the change needed, nothing will ever stay long enough. Not even yourself. I wish I knew you before you became who you were.

When it comes to being with you, it consumes my greatest fears and doubts about life. There is nothing left of me but each part that loves you and hopes you become an extension of how you see the world and it sees your soul. I hope to learn each day that begs to say your name. You are the magic underneath all the bones and misfortune I had been buried with. Regardless of where you find yourself, someone is always willing to be something you have never had, and to me, there is not anything as special and rare in this world. There is nothing more precious than another human, being human, with someone who forgot how to walk around in his or her flesh. It may take me a while to figure out, but there will be no trace of you anywhere in my life once I am done burning you out.

In all of my travels, I still hope it is you whom I find. I still hope you are there when words become useless when attempting to express these feelings of mine. I am an aging man, my eyes still have tears left from my childhood, from a time when love chased me, only to turn around and find no one to hold. There is still time for us, darling. You have always been the missing hands I have needed to touch my skin so I could finally feel love in not only the softest form, but an honest love behind their intent. I look to you the same way I view the moon. I hope you can feel each glance and lovingly stare when I am surrounded by my anxiety and depression. I love you more than they pretend to care about my life when they leave me for something better, something they can destroy. As long as I have you, my wholeness will never be ruined by their proximity to who we become.

Eventually, you are going to have to start living for yourself. We give humans too much credit for making us feel a certain way. There comes a time when you have to and need to accept reality and move on. Relationships, friendships, family issues, anything that disrupts your flow must be removed before it takes you with it. You need to do better than accepting excuses, when you know they will never change. Truth be told, the only thing we are deserving of, is what we let go of and hold onto after it is all said and done. After that, we must replant ourselves with the curiosity of which comes from pain. It comes from the mud of our sorrows, but beauty still grows.

Some people only want love because they read about it or see it and think they can do the same thing. After the trying is over, they forget what is next and end up in a lifetime of heartache and misery simply because they believed in someone else's love and not the one they had kept for themselves. Not all hands can keep fragile things from breaking. Some of us are only born with fists for war.

I know love and all its versions. I know where you are, another will find me. My hands have held the sun without burning. My heart is yours if you need it. Learning to be beside you is a life I will keep safe.

It was unexpected, me meeting you and the moon that night.
There has been a strange emptiness inside of me since that time.
Sometimes, for beautiful things to happen, you must lose
everything, including yourself. You must lose everything,
including the love you thought you were fighting for.

I want to love you well and beyond the attempts others have shown you. I honestly do not believe in a lot of things anymore, but giving your best to someone because you can, is one of them. I will never think differently about it, even if goodbye becomes you, at least there was something good about saying, I love you, that made me feel as if I belonged to something for the first time in my life.

www.ingramcontent.com/pod-product-compliance
Lightning Source LLC
Chambersburg PA
CBHW011151290426
44109CB00025B/2570